Footprints

Also by Richard Jackson

Poems
Part of the Story
Worlds Apart
Alive All Day
Svetovi Narazen (Slovenia)
Heart's Bridge (Limited Edition)
Heartwall
Half Lives
Unauthorized Autobiography
Resonance
Retrievals
Resonancia (Barcelona)
Out of Place
Traversings (with Robert Vivian)
Broken Horizons
Where The Wind Comes From
The Heart as Framed: New & Select Poems

Translations
Last Poems: Selected Poems of Pascoli (Italian, with Susan Thomas,
Deborah Brown)
Potovanje Sonca (Journey of the Sun) by Alexsander Persola (Slovene)

Chapbooks
Falling Stars
Fifties
Cesare Pavese: The Woman in the Land (translation)
Greatest Hits 1980-2004
Strays

Criticism
The Dismantling of Time in Contemporary American Poetry
Acts of Mind: Interviews with Contemporary Poets

Edited Anthologies
The Fire Under The Moon: Contemporary Slovene Poetry
Double Vision: Four Slovenian Poets (with Aleš Debeljak)
A Bridge of Voices (online e-book, with Barbara Carlson)
*The Heart's Many Doors: American Poets Respond to Metka Krašovec's
Images Responding to Emily Dickinson*

Edited Books
Tomaž Salamun, Ko vdre senca/When the Shadow Breaks
Iztok Osojnik: Selected Poems
Iztok Osojnik, Wagner (co-editing with others)

Footprints

Poems

Richard Jackson

Press 53
———•———
Winston-Salem

Press 53, LLC
PO Box 30314
Winston-Salem, NC 27130

First Edition

Cover art, "Untitled," Copyright © 2024 by Terri Harvey.
Used by permision of the artist.

Cover design by Sebastian Matthews
www.sebastianmatthews.com/art

Library of Congress Control Number
2024952296

ISBN 978-1-950413-90-4

to Terri and to my former and current students

You develop an intense global consciousness, a people orientation,
an intense dissatisfaction with the state of the world,
and a compulsion to do something about it.

—Edgar Mitchell, sixth man to walk on the moon

There's a crack in everything, that's how the light gets in.

—Leonard Cohen, "Anthem"

. . . detecting and reacting only to a small
sliver of what is going on.

—Ed Young, *An Immense World*

ACKNOWLEDGMENTS

JOURNALS

About Place Journal   Nocturne
                                             Cottonmouth

Brilliant Corners   Not Facing It
                                             Forget Keats

Cutthroat: A journal of the Arts   Bread
                                             Ghost Forests
                                             The Cottonmouth Speaks
                                             Trickster
                                             Inside the Story
                                             Poem Begun on the Day
                                             Gaza Elegy
                                             The Watchman's Fear

Ilanot Review   Your Internet Connection
                                                 Is Unstable

Jewish Literary Journal   The Layers

Michigan Quarterly Review   Contraband Camp

North American Review   The Crows of Borodyanka
                                             Footprints: Eight Tracks

Smartish Pace   Inside the Story

Symposium   Odd Radio Circles

Vita Poetica   Finding Paradise at River
                                                 Pretty, Missouri
                                             Elegy Trying to be a Psalm

ANTHOLOGIES

CONTENTS

I

AN UNHAPPY MOON

II
FOOTPRINTS: EIGHT TRACKS

III
AGAINST OUR WINTERS

I

AN UNHAPPY MOON

For night and day are mixed up here, there's mass warring everywhere,
The whole world's at loggerheads. A blasphemous battle,
As when, night from the ready chariot totters on its track
Until the driver has no hope of holding the reins and is swept away
By the team that ignores him, wildly out of control.

—Virgil, *Georgics* I, 510 ff

I believe that this world, which seems ever more filled with war, violence, extreme social injustice and bigotry, with nationalisms, racial and religious groups attempting to wheel themselves into their own narrow identities, and to fight against each other, is not the only world possible. And in this, perhaps I am not alone.

—Carlo Rovelli, *There are Places in the World Where Rules are Less Important than Kindness*

PROLOGUE TO THE UNSPOKEN POEM

The vast now consists of the form of the mental
images of whatever else we make of whatever else is
happening in the world right now. . ."
　　　　　—William Eddington, *The Rigor of Angels*

From star to star the mental optics rove,
Measure the sky and range the realms above.
There in one view we grasp the mighty whole.
　　　　　—Phyllis Wheatley, "On Imagination"

Let's just make the music of one big country tonight.
　　　　　—Wayne Shorter

Everything we see is a foothold towards what we don't see.

Like trying to gather stars from the surface of a lake.

There's a galaxy without stars, J0613+52, that resembles
a surfboard, or a cigar, or a pencil—

　　　　　　　　　　　　maybe a message from
the gods.
　　　　　Here, that woodpecker's tapping feels like code
I need to decipher, or not.
　　　　　　　　　　It resembles the distant sound
of rifle fire.
　　　　Or not.
　　　　　　　　　What we observe is not nature but
nature exposed to our method of questioning (Heisenberg).

What is the sea? The sea is a forehead wrote the poet
Tomaž Šalamun in this last book, *Kiss The Eyes of Peace.*

Where does any poem come from?
　　　　　　　　　　　　We can't know the *Now*
unless it embraces a history that is filled with questions
about its future.
　　　　　Thus, each line here worries through
its rear view mirror.

During the war the various and many
inventive tortures made a catalogue carefully ordered by
various body parts.
                    Memory walks ahead of me.

Jazz is *memory plus improvisation* said Joe Henderson.

I love the sweet sound of Ben Webster who also picked
fights in bars.
                    You can hear him breathing over the notes.

My father's favorite, Glenn Miller, was shot down over
the English Channel.

                         As was his own brother, Bernard.
The trouble with all these fragments is when you try
to piece them together.
                         Chaos theory is science's rejoinder
to our attempts to make connections with our dreams.

Just to escape some of this I take walks but too often
find myself on our Civil War battlefield.
                                        Yesterday
I stumbled on the fur of a rabbit some hawk left behind.

See, the call of the jay just out of sight is not always
an invitation to follow.
                         The difficulty is trying to fit
together the pieces.
                    According to Carlo Rovelli
the universe is granular and held together by loops.

Each image here tries to pick the lock of the next.

The war I saw in Bosnia is the same as in Ukraine.

Missiles pencil the air with incomplete messages.

The tenor Saxophonist, Sonny Rollins, wrote that
I've always considered myself a work in progress.

There's an asteroid torn from the dark side of the moon,
Kamo'oalewa, a name derived from a Hawaiian creation
chant.
       In Rovenky they burn Ukrainian literature
in local boiler rooms.
            Here they burn them to save
children from the reality they can't face.
                  Some mirrors
are swamps.
       Some souls swoop like vultures over
their own hearts.
         But the meteors keep falling nonetheless.
Everything is distant.
        I is another (Rimbaud), so
why all the hate?
         Once, in some other woods,
a fox stopped to stare at me before trotting off into
lengthening shadows measuring the time we've left.

The earth's spin is slowing which means our days
are getting longer.
        It doesn't mean the dawn's light
will seed the earth with hope.
          Time's arrow follows
a crooked path.
        Everything testifies to something beyond
itself, each step a promise, a warning or a stumble.

At the end of *By Bye Blackbird* you can hardly
recognize the melody that Coltrane has morphed.

There are moments when time turns its back
on us.
             My heart skips a beat I can't recover.

An egret lifts suddenly from the water and
our lives ripple out away from us.
                              The photo
of the woman lighting a candle in the basement
of the Church of All Saints as sounds and vibrations
of shelling in Bahkmut . . .
                    Rifle butts instead
of firewood, a blood-soaked shirt for a flag.
                                   How often
hate mugs our prayers or picks the locks of our hearts.

In Odilon's drawing a man reaches into his chest
trying to grasp his own missing heart.
                              As I write
that, somewhere a cowbird will fill an abandoned nest.

We find a gap in history and fill it with our fictions.

How often our windows frame the wrong scene.

In his travels Marco Polo mistook a rhino for a unicorn.

Columbus mistook sea lions for mermaids.
                              Mistake:
originally from the Old Norse, *taka*, "to commit
an offense," and Old English *tacan*, "to take, sieze,"
which tells us how often what we don't see or know
leads to tragedy.

                    Still, it is the only way to know
what we don't know,
                              for every first step is always
a mistake.
                    Language tells us nothing that is new.

Maybe we should remake ourselves as verbs.

Only the chasm in each word tells us the truth.

The woman who went to the well to fill
her pitcher enters a space where she was not.

We'll be together again, Ben Webster ends *'Round Midnight.*

This is why we can only be everywhere we are not.

It is why we must embrace ourselves in the other.

Each vision a parallel world, each world its own
intangible presence, each presence an embrace.

It is what lets the poem or score gather its stars for eternity.

Each note creates an horizon the next must expand,
leaving behind an emptiness only love can fill.

In Kharkiv the emptiness fills the souls of everyone.

It blossoms like those starless galaxies being born,
gathering clouds and pieces of dark matter into
a whole so far beyond what we know but what
we must learn to believe.

For that Bluejay there, each
call is a pathway it follows like a shooting star.

For Composer Wayne Shorter, music was religion.

These are echoes of belief and doubt we try to fathom.

And what poem does not believe it can walk on water?

THE CROWS OF BORODYANKA

The day itself seems to tremble as if from a tank's
vibration. But they have left except for a few charred
hulks.
     A few shadows lumber across the streets as if
their clouds denied them.
               But it's the crows waiting
in the skeletal trees for the dogs to finish that is the focus
here. They know.
         They do not pray to any god or star.
They just know.
         They sit with a silence that catches
on the throat of the sky,
           like drones recording the cyclist
shot dead, the woman carrying what's left of her life
in a sack.
        Left for weeks the bodies grow to twice
their size.
        There's enough left so the crows don't need
to argue.
        Meanwhile, they note the roof slabs leaning
against the honeycomb shells of former buildings
like tombstones,
         the red and yellow swing set standing
amidst the rubble.
          In Kyiv, Father Balog says it's Christ
who is also raped and tortured. Crucified again.

I think the crows know where the mines are buried.

Even Earendil, twenty-eight billion light years away
must know what the stench means.
               The day trembles
like a solar wind through the universe.
                  Nowhere to hide.

A few bayonets of light cut through the ruins.

Our few tortured words are never enough.

They lay around like unexploded shells.

I would have to learn the language of crows to understand.

PHOTO: OMARSKA CAMP, BOSNIA, 1992

Night had snuck through the barbed wire perimeter.

This could be Auschwitz. This could be Ukraine or
the gulag.
        Moonlight bled into the surrounding clouds.

You could barter a button for a piece of bread.

In those days other countries would hide beneath
convenient slogans.
        Not much has changed.

Sometimes the shadows of missing relatives wandered
the yard.
        The men stood around in clouds made of breath.

There were many unused rooms in their hearts.

How easy it is to count the ribs of the men clutching
the fence for the photographer,
        and how impossible
it is to feel what they felt.
        Here the sky is hopelessly lost.

We get the news from one unreliable source, or another.

Things are said to be *unclear* which mean we don't know
but won't admit it.
        Truth holds on like a flood survivor
on a rooftop.
        The most important words were given
new meanings.
        Tattered dreams were weighed down
by stories no one believed.

Flood lights stalked the fences.

At every horizon, history hopelessly waited to speak.

Now, decades later, these images continue to haunt.

The path a bullet takes stays frozen in the air for decades.

The whole story could be told today by the young boy
kicking a ball across the yard that is no longer there.

In the end our stories keep circulating with our blood.

Under the stones beyond the camp there are still
gaunt and starving stories that think they have escaped.

LAYERS

Jewish Ghetto, Rome

He's under his own shell, next to the Turtle Fountain
where a single ray of light seems to write a text
on his orange tent, a scene Dante would have
evoked.
        A Few blocks away the Nazis rounded up
whole generations for their own inferno.
                                Cacere
is the word they stole from him, though *prison* was
what they meant.
                Bernini created the fountain
to remember the history the Jews have carried
on their backs.
                Can the children circling it now
on cobblestone outrun their own history?

The Romans knew this place as a deadly swamp.

The fading siren sounds carry another kind of
history.
        The storefront oranges and artichokes carry
a history longer than any of this.
                        Someone just said
she felt ghosts sweeping through here.
                                My own
ghosts are here to meet them.
                        We are all looking
for a way out of history.
                        I think those circling children
keep returning to begin anew.
                        This is how time
becomes space, the words we walk through
creating an ever expanding, ever receding
horizon,
        the history we create each time we write,
hoping to escape the prisons of our own ghosts.

                for Amir Or

GAZA ELEGY

With words of sacred scripture
I shield the oranges from phosphorous.
—Hiba Abu Nada (24 June 1991 to 20 October 2023)

October's waxing moon attempting to embrace
Venus as she rises from dusk's ashes.
                              Instead,
cosmic dust gathering in the heart's corners.

The whole sky turning away
                              and the lake here
refusing to reflect it.
                    A world of blind birds
shattering the windows into fractals with
names that open like prison doors—*The scars on our*
children's faces will look for you (Mosad Abu Toha)

but find instead splintered apartment complexes, bombed
refugee camps, bits of people that can't be re-assembled.

Each word a telescope, each breath a microscope,
each love a hyphen.
                              What is out of sight hijacks
the truth.
                    Memories mold in a mind's eternal
dusk.
            A crescent moon offers no consolation,
nor does the child's notebook with it burnt edges.

Yet how easily here the geese and ducks have settled
by the pond together,
                              and how easily we name
dumb bombs or *smart bombs* as if they had
a mind of their own and not our own mindings.

How many spirits are still living in ruins that speak
stories no one wants to hear, no one wants to see.

Does a dead star still claim what light abandoned it?

Do all futures have to be recurrent tragedies?

There aren't enough sheets to cover all the bodies.

No scream is loud enough. A blind cosmos floats away.

BREAD

For Maria, her photo in Ternopil Oblast, Ukraine

It looks like you're standing in your kitchen before
a dozen loaves of Palyanitsa,

           saints as they are called,
for citizen soldiers.

          I've watched my own wife
knead and wad bread as if somehow she was
shaping a world that had yet to be imagined
or remembered.

         I imagine the mourning doves,
Holub zhaloby, pecking at the crumbs just beyond
your frame.

       Maybe they are the same doves
that landed on the hands of the priest in Kharkiv
as the shells and rockets landed around him.

             Here
the doves are scrambling to find a few seeds beneath
the light snow covering. They know nothing of your war.

Or do they? I saw the same doves around the rubble
in Bosnia, the same near Split.

          Light stammered through
heaps of ruins there as if it wanted to say something.

How much does a shadow weigh, a girl once asked
in Bosnia, in another war like yours, how much space
does a heart occupy, she added.
         I thought then
how the body shrinks, how our lives starve on the way
to their own emptiness.
        It is your *saints* that sustain us.

Though far from you, the air strike on a bread factory
in Makariv killed thirteen fellow bakers and tells us
what you mean to us.
                            It is impossible to feel what
they felt, or you feel, though we try with words
that have no real translation.

                            And what is the heart
anyway, but a wadded ball of half written poems?

CONFESSIONAL

One terror catapults over the last.

                           On a night the owls
fear to ask questions.

                   Family photos filling the smoke
like flies.

           Svetlana Kostrykina rolling her husband's riddled
body back home in a wheelbarrow, his arms flopping
over the side, first light creeping over Kyiv rooftops
meaning danger.

               Garbage piled on top of the other bodies.

The light from stars looking for a detour.

                          Even after
your skull explodes something in you must hear the shot.

Not insects but the low clank of distant tanks.

The distant morning seems a hoax.

                      Four soldiers
in neat uniforms and Nubuck boots passing
around a bottle.

          Easy shot—her husband
on his cell phone.

          Curious pigeons at his head.

Above it all, only the shredded tent of the sky.

Holed up in the cellar, you'd need a calendar to keep
track of the days,

          you'd need a mirage to count
the window boxes full of fresh flowers,

               but how
else to keep track of the bodies fast becoming
mere headlines or news spots?

How easy it would be
to name them here where the future's bodies
are stripped for valuables,
                              where our own
memories sit down beside us for a nervous smoke,
maybe even put down their wine glasses to speak
the truth.
            The reflection in the store window is
not always ours, powerless as ever—

puppets whose strings have been cut.

ODD RADIO CRCLES (ORCS)

Our hot-air balloon / turned into a lead ball.
—Marjana Savka, Ukrainian poet

They look like a virus you'd see under a microscope.

A city flattened by artillery.

A bubble with a galaxy inside it, an amorphous shroud.

Not unlike the bubbles a child blows waiting in line for bread.

Undulating as if in waves towards an absent shore.

Carrying the driftwood of space and time.

Only seeing what the radio telescope writes on film.

Like what is hidden in the pictures from Mariupol

Beyond me, waves of forest sounds I can't decipher.

The sky netted in the top branches.

The moles, even, afraid to show themselves for the cat.

The sun rises, scraping the top of the ridgeline.

What it sees: the 18-month-old girl, head blown open by shrapnel.

A forest of excuses. A land too far.

The smell of the fox the hunter skinned and abandoned.

The burning stumps loggers leave.

You can't make the days follow your calendar, or the streets follow your maps.

You can tell each country on them by its color.

A country, a puddle on the map. (Lyudmyla Khersonska)

16-year-old Iliya, whose legs were sheared off during a soccer game.

These names fall in like mortar rounds.

The wind here tonight, as if the trees were screaming.

The animal paths written through brambles.

Time drifts away in smoke.

Someone's pajamas with cartoon unicorns in the ruins.

Each line a radio wave, a bomb's shock wave.

Even the sky looks metallic, its stars aiming at us.

The scalloped clouds above me appearing as flack puffs.

In Mariupol they can hear the missiles overhead.

The vapor trails linger longer than their bombs.

The coyote the other day carried some small creature in its jaws.

Just some scattered white fur after the owl dove in.

Dogs scavenging. A maternity ward become a morgue.

Death, the empty parentheses.

The empty web quivering along the trail yesterday.

Nouns with betraying modifiers.

To erase the names on the maps, to clear-cut the lives.

Now we know: Cambrian tribolites ate each other.

Twenty-three species went extinct last year. We aren't yet among them.

A world where we once lived has left us words. (Serhiy Zhadan)

ORCS are either eating of being eaten by galaxies like ours.

Who beyond the cosmos is watching us?

The freeze fog here has crumpled the day lilies.

The oak that fell last year is riddled with insect holes.

Kudzu is strangling our trees.

The racoons are at the garbage. There is no food in Mariupol.

In the theater, pieces of children scattered among the dead.

The building just folded in on itself. A black hole.

Here, at least, the clouds can escape over the ridgeline.

ORCS are one billion light years away, further than
        the Black Hole that will someday consume us.

How long does it take to consume a city?

What species does not kill its own to live? To rule?

The answers open like craters.

The last mass extinction was only the fifth to date.

Today the doomsday clock is set at under two minutes.

A disease looking for any opening.

Hearts with nothing left to pump.

Someone mentioned that roots dig downwards to escape us.

The moon slowly eaten by its own shadow.

In all this, a few birds create their own space to fly through.

In the child's drawing they look like angels.

A man with a wheelbarrow carrying away his life.

The whole city still giving birth to prayers.

Mariupol means the city of Mary.

Shrouds of smoke. Hope hides in the underbrush.

This litany of salvaged images.

How seldom we decipher the signals from our own words.

A city crumples like a map in a commander's hand.

The day ends like a burnt-out car.

INSIDE THE STORY

New Liberty Cemetery,
Graysville, Ga, May 19, 2023

Inside the distant clouds the past and future exchange
silent blows—like fireflies trapped in a spider's web,—
the day's light sifting down into the evening light.

Inside that purple light lies Graysville, and inside that,
the New Liberty Cemetery with its geometric lines
of polished stones,
        and inside that, beyond the fence,
the weathered stones hunched over as if still working
the fields,
        and inside that, alongside the overgrown
trees and years of dead leaves, lies the grave of
Mattie Green, her story,
        and inside that, the bombing,
night of May 23, 1960, Ringgold, Georgia, a few miles
south,
        on a clearer night than this, the guilty stars seeming
to cascade down like water over the horizon, a bomb
set off under the house, under her bed, without suspects,

though inside that, Christmas Eve, 1865, Pulaski, Tennessee,
seven men don the first hoods at the office of Judge Jones,

and inside that, and inside that—
        but here, now, I hear
the White Breasted Nuthatch quiver with the leaves
of the maple as if to counter the coming storm
at the end of this day that does not know it is dying,

finding shelter in a blueprint of bramble from a hawk
scything over the town's guilt faster than I can name her,

sounding, I imagine, the name of Mattie Green, 32 years old,
on this night when the stones have begun to lift themselves up,

because to tell her story is to listen to the light of fireflies,
this night where her story is opening inside all our stories.

DNIPRO ELEGY

In Dnipro, time is the drone stalking an apartment house.

Each day the clocks are rewound.
                              The drone's wash
is barely a hum.
                    What's left is a rumor of buried voices.
The air turns the color of those cries.
                              A layer of dust
serves as the only body bags.
                         How quickly concrete
turns to dust.
                 There are unspoken adjectives in what
I need to say.
                 The earth tilts on its axis as if to lend
an ear to what we never hear.
                              Who listens when we speak?
The light lies limply on the ruins.
                              Everything that is missing
stays missing.
                 Every track leaves its own emptiness.

Any elegy about this will need sutures.
                              Any metaphor
for this reveals its own lie.
                         A few parts of concrete
walls stand like grotesque memorials.
                              Still, a few birds
return, perched next to the sun on a barren tree limb.

Maybe it's true, as the philosophers say, what is outside us
comes from what is inside,
                         as if our words could send out
new beginnings
                 the way mushrooms create their own
breeze to disperse their spores,

                  or the way stardust drifts
through space to form new lives,
                  but in the end, maybe
the hope is that, as Miles Davis said, *don't play
what's there, play what's not there,*
                  desperately hoping
for that last pocket of air left in the wordless rubble.

GRAVITY

There's always a gap in our own story which is the
soul's emptiness
      like the open door on a passing
freight train,
     the hole in the screen,
         the mouth of
the vole's abandoned burrow,
       or Jesus' empty tomb.

Those scorched birds falling into the emptying
forest of the western fires,
       leaving their unanswered calls
drifting with the smoke
      like those mist-like
constellations whose light is torn every which way
by the earth's gravitational field,
        which some
scientists say looks like a deformed tomato.

It's what shapes our stories—
       Magritte's surreal
men falling stiffly at attention into Golconda,
or his Castle of the Pyrenees sitting on a rock
in pure space.
     It's gravity after all, which falls
to us from the Old French *gravitas*, but also *grave*,
meaning where we are headed, and the serious
thought which it engraves on our hearts.

It must have been that way for the Italian
soldiers who tried to defy gravity and fell
among the icy rock crevices on the mountains
at Kobarid, Slovenia in 1919,
       and were found
because the seeds of the tomato plants they were
saving for Spring sprouted from their pockets.

The story of the Confederate Rose has an hibiscus
taking on the blood of a fallen soldier is an allegory
about resurrection.
                    That fateful morning, as Venus
signaled its own mysteries, as the first light was
stirring in the dirt,
                    how many actually approached
the tomb
              and why forget the story they were told?

Before they could report, the stars had dissolved,
the heavens seemed more distant.
                              If the cosmos
keeps expanding does it create the empty space
it will grow into?
                  The emptiness between stars is
terrifying.
              Every story has its own black hole.

Unicorn, the closest Black Hole to earth could
someday abscond with all our stories.
                                    It is no
mythical creature but has been hiding in plain
sight all this time.
                  How do you believe what
you do not see or hear except by some leap
of faith
          like the woman who went to the well
to fill her pitcher, fnding a story she could believe.

One night, hearing stories of yet another war,
we watched the meteors, attracted by our own
gravity, streak like tracer rounds,
                                  like embers
from a campfire,
                  like fireflies signaling
each other,

as we each called out a metaphor,
until someone remembered how it was

gravity the leapers at the World Trade Center
trusted more than flames as they fell among

the remarkable red mist that filled the air above
the burst bodies of the other leapers,
                                        so many
leaping backwards out of the flames, holding
hands,
          facing the sky as if they might imagine

themselves sitting in some open field, thinking of

the embers and mist as fireflies in their desperate
attempt to imitate the stars,
                              or grasping handfuls
of wind as the floor windows passed like a broken film,

for to remember that is to remember every leap of love
made of everything that falls,
                              everything that flies off,

as in the film of that one bird leaping phoenix-like above
the burning western spruce,
                              which is also the leap
we make with our own stories trying to surmount
the chasms of our own hearts and souls, imagining

the unknowable prayers of the leapers, left in mid air,
prayers sprouting like seeds of hope above the smoke.

TWO PHOTOS

1. TO A CHILD WITH MOTHER, YECHILA, ETHIOPIA

The world is joyless for a while
—Pablo Pusterla

It must be a classroom, the blackboard as vacant
as the desks that lean against the wall, their empty
drawers facing us, open mouthed, as if they too
were searching for food.
                      I have no answers for
what you must be asking.
                      I have no way to know
what you feel except what is in my own heart.

That is never enough.
                      Soldiers from Eritrea have
ravaged the town.
                      Your hand to your mouth,
like your mother behind you, are you wondering
what to do next? Where to go?
                      Outside, the land
doesn't seem real, but rather like the sepia tint of
an old photo.
                Shadows still walk the streets.

A few cow carcasses stretch beyond the town.

And your mother, she seems to watch how the sun
has begun to rise, it's light starting to streak
across the wall and blackboard,
                      wondering
if it is safe to step outside, if she can begin again,
if she can erase the images lodged in your heart.

2. BOY PEERING BEHIND A WALL, AMHARA, ETHIOPIA

a miraculous story, but everyone hurries to believe it
                            —Jane Hirshfield

He's watching Timkat, the remembrance of the baptism of
Jesus, the villagers, out of the photo, splashing in a pool,
baptizing their souls,
                      their past,
                                  their hopes for a future
of food as available as the incalculable stars above them.

But his mother behind him is pregnant with child and with fear.

The Kalashnikov of the soldier beside them reminds us of
the terrors that went from house to house raping and stealing.

Does that explain the mother's condition?
                                  The fighting has
lasted decades.
              A few church forests have survived despite
the stripped trees from artillery hits that dot the rest of the
rusted earth.
              The mother is holding what appears to be a few
stalks of grain and a tiny bag for what will be their supper.

Legend has it, the hills beyond the photo have been scraped
clean by the hand of Qaynan, the god of war and destruction.

The boy's face tells us he has already understood *tree, water,
earth, war, famine.*
                      He must wonder why the villagers rejoice,
how they must know more than he does,
                                  more than we can,
more than I can write here,
                          what it means in this age of endless
wars, to hope, to praise, to sing the songs they learned from trees.

CONTRABAND CAMP

*African Americans, freedmen and ex-slaves, were considered
contraband under the Confiscation Act. The contraband camps
became the foundation for postwar segregated neighborhoods.
Chattanooga's camp was located on the "other side" of the Tennessee River.*
—*The Chattanoogan*, March 10, 2022

The everything that is signified in all the nothing that is there. . ..
—Gerald Early, "Lighter than Air"

It was the picture of the man crouched on the rubble in Dubrovnik,
December, nineteen ninety-one, and then this old man crouched
on the Tennessee riverbank this evening,

                         both of them holding
an empty birdcage, as if to say *at least something can be let free,*
and standing here now where the Contraband Camp stood,
looking across the river towards the glass buildings, reflecting
the late sun where pontoon guard houses once kept the two sides
apart.

       Here time mixes like the feeder streams running into the coves.
Petals of light dot the surface as they have always done.
Where once the slavers from Meigs county hunted for freedmen,
the roller skaters and skateboarders emerge from shadows like bats,
frogs still signal out their complaints to anyone who will listen.

I can't write those stanzas and not be haunted by that
other river, the Miljacka, I once crossed in Sarajevo before
that war, dividing Christians and Muslims, my friends starting to fear
each other, a fear that would later rise, and then explode with
snipers dividing the streets, vapor trails dividing the sky, words collapsing
like bombed buildings,

                        and then those refugees tossing tree limbs over
a barbed wire fence to cross over, loaded boats swamped before
reaching shore, and now that cable car suspended over the river Dnieper.

But this is Chattanooga, two thousand and twenty-three, and it is
now Renaissance Park with its paved paths, benches and tables,
its memories forged into plaques, the jonquils starting to bloom.
stars beginning to scratch the other side of the sky as if to break
through to their own freedom,

                      and while I can see the rising moon
that still flowers over Missionary Ridge, I know it brought as little hope,
then, to the contraband, as it does to me now, watching pick-ups parade
around with their confederate flags waving like the tails of wood rats
from their truck beds across the river.

                      You have to look for any sign,
Josip said on an evening like this in Sarajevo those years ago. I know
that later the clouds from an oncoming front will cut off the moon,
but for now the water taxis keep linking the two shores, the board paddlers
pass freely from one side to the other, the herons don't care which
shore they alight on.

                And yes, while there's also a storm inside us
we can't see snaking its color bands across the center of our phone
screens, dividing us from what's to come, from our own selves, and
still, yes, I am still looking for any sign-- the stars beginning to assert
themselves, the moon still rising, the swifts darting in and out of
the shadows beneath the bridge that connects the two shores, the music
of the street vendors, a river otter fingering freely between the pier posts,

and it is as if I can hear the sounds from the camp now, whispering
like words cocooned inside these words, spreading like the waters
that once flooded here, sending the contraband to higher ground, and then
the old man rising now, *love birds* is all he says, now whispered out
of sight, kindling a song against the wind, like what is written beneath
the bark of trees, how fear takes the shape of the doe slipping
out of the camera's frame, to cradle the world's ruins close
to our hearts, and that, while our own words may die,
it is those birds' music that grows in our lungs towards speech.

MIRIAM'S PROPHECY

I have become a resident foreigner in a foreign land.
              —Exodus 2:22

for *Amir Or*

While I waited in the rushes each hour seemed hostage
to the next.
              My language was cradled in hope.

Yet they soon learned it was no land of milk and honey.

Now all I hear is a bird's cry tearing at the fabric
of first light.
              All night moonlight has tilled the earth
but nothing has bloomed.
                            History seems to linger,
a wave that never breaks.
                            Listen: the geometry here
has no sides
              and the languages of all sides are filled
with defoliated words.
                            Threats hide like hidden bats
from the outstretched limbs of their sentences.

Their languages say *pacification, collateral damage,*
say Gaza or Ashkelon, say *surgical strike,* say
rich target instead of *rape* or *atrocity,* words
as infinite as *grains of sand* or *stars.*
                            Death is
not the amazing tombs of the Egyptians,
not a child-like snuggle in Abraham's bosom,
not the country of dreams Homer wrote about.

Listen, when Pharoah died, I danced to the timbrel
and played the hand drum.
                            But later my own feelings
pointed like the tip of a flame.

            Because I questioned wrongly
and was outcast for days, I know what it means to be
oppressed and homeless, afraid to have a friend, each
breath grabbing at my lungs.
                    We can't herd history into
our private pens.
                    Your own science says everything is held
together by strong and weak forces, that even dark holes
emit some kind of light, some kind of hope.
                                And yes,
isn't it the same way with us?
                            Yes, truth often seems to waver
like the Northern Lights—as if at an arm's length from reality.

Today I watched one of your sparrows return to its own
nest carrying what it had learned from distant fields.

I am called a prophet but my name in Hebrew means
a *sea of bitterness* and in Arabic, *secret knowledge*.

All I can do is continue to watch, and if you look up you will
see the migrant birds heading towards a sorrowful horizon.

VERA'S VIOLIN

On his Kobza playing,
By his songs the people know him...
For he drives away their sorrows
        —Taras Shevchenko, "Prebendya," trans. C. Manning

It's because we live on a tilted world that we don't see straight.
It is like ignoring the dark side of the moon, content with
questions that smolder in the fireplace, and answers
that take the shape of ashes that have forgotten the fire.

It is like looking through one of these windowpanes and ignoring
the rest of the window.
                        Outside the deer follow a single
trail from one frame to another. Seams of sunlight open
in the woods. A few clouds blanket the distant hills.

In the middle of writing those lines, the music of Vera Lytochenko
came from her cellar bomb shelter in Kharkiv, playing for a few
neighbors, the apartment windows above her blown out,
playing beyond the charred vehicles, beyond even the stars
that frost the sky above the roofless buildings.
                                But here I am
safely watching the meandering ground birds hunting for seed,
the top branches of the Tulip Poplar reaching out as if
to track the vapor trails of planes but never abandoning its
trunk
        and there's a false wishing well tilted like the tree that fell
last night, but it had only reminded me of the toppled minaret in
Banja Luka, shelled during that other war, from another frame.

The congregation prayed from cellars, bullet holes covered
the walls like dead stars.
                        How many people live inside stories
they never hear, histories that are gestures we offer
to the darkness.
                It's true, we are the only species that weeps.

It is our silence that leaves the emptiness of shell holes in the earth.

In truth, I had originally started this poem in anger by describing
a Pileated Woodpecker's gun firing off several rounds, and two hawks
circling us like drones,
                                but when Vera's violin entered above playing
What A Moonlit Night it was as if each note lamented the one before it.
I'll cradle you close to my heart the lyrics finally promise.
                                                        Promises.
Ashes. Stars hesitating, forgetting.
                                I remember how it was, my own heart
searching like the bird that kept flying furtively against
my grammar school window while we listened to the radio broadcast
from Budapest, 1956, as the tanks rolled in and the nuns kept
promising safety if we prayed as we hunched beneath our wooden
desks, practicing.
                        Budapest, Banka Luka, the same pictures we see
now from Karkhiv.
                        Outside my window, a woodpile, each log
decaying into the next. The moon rising like a whole note.
                                                        A few
night sounds adding their own chorus.
                                When her violin ends
I can play it again as if her dream could dream on without
her, but listening to that desperate music as it searches
for a way to live among the ruins,
                                I understand this poem's
desire to outlast its ending,
                                understand the bones of brush
kindling a song against the wind,
                                what is written beneath
the bark of trees,
                and how fear takes the shape of the doe

slipping out of the window's frame, understand that

cradling the world's ruins close to our hearts,

while our own words may fall away like radio waves,
it is her music that grows in our lungs, redeeming our speech.

SUDANESE DISPATCH

Some nights you could feel the pulse of the stars.

Every day meant hours of shade beneath the Umbrella
Thorn. Gum trees stored water against the drought.

Now the skeletons of buildings return to sand.

Soldiers from one side or another transform
Wadi Madani into a relic.
                              That is, after the usual
rapes, disembodiments, tortures against the Masalit.

The bodies of children look like deflated balloons.

In our own silence we can hear their desperate lungs'
soft whistle.
                  Dusk is already at our doors.

Time chokes on its own catalogue of atrocities.

And so I write this for Rouda who walked fifteen
days towards safety in Chad with her child,

like the Jacana bird carrying is own young,
hardly recognizing her own memories, stories
like calendars missing too many years.

YOUR INTERNET CONNECTION IS UNSTABLE

On the dead on heir backs, with their arms toss'd wide,
Pour down your unstinted nimbus, sacred moon.
                              —Whitman, Drum Taps

Even before I began there were reluctant images
on my walk across the Chickamauga Battlefield

trying to find their way out of what is to come,
though,
            like opening a folded map,
                                    one thing
follows another, like the crows circling that hawk,
attacking like fighter planes,
                              or the erratic gliders
my father helped me build those years when
he could still remember my name,
                              but how
connect all this, and what about
                                    the stink bug
crawling over a TV screen this morning
                                    where
children were playing with toy swords scripted by
one of their countless video games,
                              or those burning
images on the computer,
                        which takes me to a burnt out
house without its roof and above,
                              a hesitant moon shrouded
by lingering smoke
                  from a drone strike that has
the man leaning out from what is left of the cellar
window,
        (an image I cannot erase from this page)
sipping gorilka from a dented tin cup left over from
the last attack,
                while so many shadows are still
looking for their bodies,
                        as in the slightest wind
one can hear a few names still wandering

their old haunts,
                    calling out the names of flowers,
of birds,
            or of that one love whose impression
still waits on the blood-soaked mattress behind him

which brings us to these images trying to speak despite me:

the riverbed rocks of the bloodied Bakhmutka River,

and a pocket watch with no hands as if to say
                                        something
about how little time we have
                        as now a ripple from
a passing body washes over it,
                        how the smallest
image or memory explodes,
                        and how a curious cat
washes itself in the endless current with hardly
a glance at the watch face which meant
                                    as little to it
as those rocks streaked with minerals and history

because by this time I am wondering what else is
lurking behind these words
                        that is so hard to face,
that arrive like stray bullets,
                        or like the way
the other day, thinking of these refugee-like images,

it is impossible to say what is now and what memory,

a fear really, that my past would dissolve like my father's,

like surface roots that tease with unnamed messages,

or the wind teasing the matted leaves
                                              to reveal
what lies beneath, a wind my father called
God's Breath
                          though it was William Paley, 1802,
who said God was just a watchmaker who
winds it up and walks away,
                                              but I cannot walk away,
still trying to make connections because for me,

wondering if it is wrong to simply wonder at
the simple presence of the deer feasting on sweet grass,

or the racoon scurrying along, hardly aware of me,

or here where the regiment markers name the dead
through the crosshairs of bramble
                                              and where a coyote
had chased a shivering rabbit,
                                              because,
that image of the drone over Backhmut
hunting for hidden trenches and foxholes

and maybe for that man,
                                              still leaves the problem: to decipher
what all these flashing images have to do with me,—

for I feel like my father in his last years when
a few pigeons rose up like a dream
                                              and he raised
a few syllables for words he could not find,
staring off to where
                          he must still be wandering
in our old woods,
                          refusing to hunt,
                                              even after
years in his own war,

                   puzzling over the path
that brought him there,
                   or maybe these woods,
whose trails are crossed by spider filaments,

whose fields are lined with bales of hay
in the shape of cannon wads,
                   images that keep
bringing me back to Bakhmut
                while they
already start to sign out of this poem,
losing all connection,
              like first stars from
the beginning of the cosmos now almost
too far to see even with the Hubble scope, but still
connecting us to our own beginnings,
                 and to those
Ukraine deaths too far to understand,
                  too close not
to feel, and I remember how in Virgil's *Aeneid*,
a king, needing to carry his infant over a river,
ties her to a spear and throws her across,
                  allowing
Virgil's poem to continue,
             which gives me time
here to connect these settings, trying desperately,

while the cicadas underground are already preaching
their own deaths,
             time to pray for what is happening
to a river town
          which is the point here, after all,

time to remember a man, taking his solitary watch
at his cellar window,
             in a present he calls the future
and for a father whose future was buried in his past.

NOT THE POEM

Don't write what you know, write what you don't know.
—Toni Morrison

Just to poke around in the images strewn about
by the Isklander missile that landed in Kramatorsk,
mobs of words pressing against
a reality that longer feels real,

words that mean nothing to Hannah Valeriivna,
a school principal, nothing to the children being
fitted for flak jackets
rearranging their future

where their roads unravel like barbed wire,
where their dreams are translated into rifle fire,
their horizons receding,
life turning into metaphors.

Listen, there is the life we live in our poems and
the life without. There is the emptiness between
one page and another,
one life and another.

Still, one word attracts another like the invisible
tug of the moon. Nothing exists by itself. As I
write this, a green comet is
approaching as it has done

every fifty thousand years linking us in some way to
ancestors we can never know, as every day I have lived
has also been coming to
this moment, this page,

whose idiom is silence, the sound of wind stopping,
our local coyote stopping to sample the air, the silence
of that missile before
it strikes, words

comprised of letters after Z, words that can't mean but
hope to embrace, even if as large as the emptiness
that rests in the
charred crater

in the middle of Kramatorsk, something we can never really
name, only recall the fault lines these feelings leave, these
pencil scratches scattered like
so much debris, dear Hannah.

STORIES FROM THE SOIL

These unstable side streets.
These tired angry confused answers.
—Earl Braggs, "A Love letter from George Jackson to Angela Davis"

Evening, the sky turning rust. A last moth wanders into
the path of a passing bat.
                              Further out, a few stars are
born while others die.
                      Atlanta, September 22, 1906,
rumors spreading like ground fog. The air riddled with
cries.
        The horse carts seem frozen.
                                      Annie Shepherd
shot in the chest at close range.
                                  Everything is close
and distant in this desert country of the heart.
                                                  One
of two hundred and fifty stories.
                                On her way from work.
No one notices the first stars,
                            just the constellations of
men and boys with their guns.
                              From the Forsyth Bridge
bodies meteor to the ground.
                            Decades later the heart's
sky still turns rust.
                    If there is a word for this, I do not
know it.
        New stories still billow among the clouds.
                                                  Here,
I watch the morning rise like an unanswerable question.

The birds take turns at the feeder.
                                    They have no need
to ask forgiveness.
                  Syllables, scattered about like seed,
are trying to find a way.
                        The syntax of years still feels
undecipherable.
              The hands of the clock still slip backwards.

CLEOPAS' WARNING

Emmaus

After three days every twig looked like a snake.
No one could really say what we were seeing.
The dust from the *Khamison* wind would have been
enough, but that wasn't it. Who, then, wanted
to look straight at anyone? There were always signs,
but what did they mean? I am making no excuses.
We all invent our own scenes from the shadows
that creep around the corners of our eyes. You
yourselves have elected the antichrist who claims
to be 'the chosen one.' What they thought was
my house has become a church. How real is anything?
So many words and dates have passed over
that road. Here and there some shade from
pine or olive, but we couldn't rest for fear of being
asked. It wasn't the darkness but the silence we feared.
He spoke, yes, and we should have known Him.
Each memory is covered by another memory.
You have to see infinity in a grain of sand, as Blake
wrote, and eternity in an hour. You are not going to
find heaven in some telescope. It was only when
we ate that we knew, though I am not sure exactly
what He said, only how he said it, something like
an embrace. So. It is not enough just to know a snake
from a stick. Take that man, chalking a sign to hold
at the crossroads. Who really knows who he is?
And those black holes you search the far skies for,
are you sure that they're not some distant galaxy,
but hidden, unrecognized, in your own hearts?

THE COTTONMOUTH SPEAKS

I love to watch the owl rip the seams of darkness
trying to find me. Like a broom, he sweeps up
whatever I leave him—frogs, fish, voles, anything
not to my taste.
                After night drops its mask I'm off.
I prefer what you call the "swamp" though I will
never admit it.
              There are no straight lines, or stories.

I leave my skins for you to decipher—each word
you invent for them is quicksand, each idea
a trip mine.
            As with mermaid weed, crowsfoot,
cobra fern, you name things hoping they are
something else.
             Take me at my word. Don't ever
excuse me.
             Even young, we learned to entrap
you with a simple ambiguous tale. My own eyes
change shape from day to night.
                  Our secret is:
Eden is our playbook, and in time you'll see I am
your *redeemer*, I am your *retribution*.
                    We know
ourselves as the Elect.
           We have our own facts.

We too have a kind of militia.
                  What they say
about us is fake news—we do not swarm
to attack you.
           In fact, we'll eat each other
when times are tough just to stay ahead of you.

Watch where you step, your ideals are no defense.

We rely on your myths the way you rely
on your religion,
     for we have learned so well
that you cannot twist the truth you do not know,
as one of your poets tells you.
       Your logic will
end up biting you in the end.
       And what is
the brain but carrion corrupted into worms,
as your Jonathan Swift wrote, and the soul
just a deflated balloon.
      I am already on
the move for only I can lead the way.

A vine climbs to the side of the oak
like an extra spine, trying to imitate me.

You'll think I am a floating twig until too late.

At which time I will eat the sound of your fear.

VINNYTSIA, JULY 13, 2022

Just before, the Tawny Pipit froze in its song,
the ravens fled in a single shadow.
                                    The buzzing
of flies, the butterfly that would be blown across
the square.
                    Before a child called "Sunny Flower,"
pushed her tram into this moment
                                    when across the square
someone lights his fourth morning cigarette.

That is just at 10:45, when people separate from
their shadows.
                    The Kabr arrives like a line drawn
across a sheet of paper. This paper.
                                    No. It's dust
dancing in those shadows.
                                    Strips of metal hang
everywhere like leaves.
                            What she understood
was only a flash of color like her dye paintings saying
Look at me, alive, please.
                        Sunlight bleeds
across the square.
                    That awful moment just after,
its emptiness.
                    Someone has moved the pram
to a grass island.
                    How many lives drift in the smoke
with her.
            What a waste the world is,
wrote Trakl.
            We are all guilty, wrote St. Paul.

Smoke smudges the sun.
                            In the distance the pain
of church bells.
                  The light itself wavers and topples.

Shadows search for their shadows.
                                  The heart,
the heart is a hornet's nest of these memories.

POEM BEGUN ON THE DAY I BEGAN ANOTHER YEAR

Chattanooga, Rome

And then what? Just these words floating around
like bits of dust showing themselves only at the first
     light that grazed the trees on the frayed ridge line?
     Like garbled messages on the answering machine?

Beyond the window where the Mockingbird had
watched me, a few clouds were dragging themselves
     to whatever came next. The oak's branches reaching
     out hoping to fill the void that keeps growing.

A gecko vanishing suddenly into the rubble of
a stone wall. The mockingbird not saying anything.
     Each word is more frail than what it names.
     I want my shadow to take a step beyond itself.

I learned just now that an owl will take a squirrel whole.
I could hear a few sirens pass through McCallie tunnel,
     earlier a few shots blistered the air.
     We were taught to pray in such moments.

So many stories sift through the sieve of possibility
or burrow into their own burrows. On that day
     five souls in Colorado Springs woke, their hours
     threading their way towards some pattern

they wouldn't recognize for two days. *You can't understand,*
someone says, *you are not them. I see, not feel,* wrote Coleridge,
     but he too was wrong. *To feel,* from Old English to *touch,*
     and Old Norse, *to reach for.* Here it's the Italian, *sento.*

I am trying to find words that branch out beyond my own story,
that fumble trough their own darkened tunnels.
     We are part of all possible worlds, wrote David Lewis.
     Each knows. They know every day ends before it ends.

This is why these words have no words for themselves, why
they embrace each other the way these five cormorants
          have risen together from the Tiber leaving empty shadows
          behind, riding as one soul, and yes, the way
          those five souls, with all our souls, have entered here.

II

FOOTPRINTS: EIGHT TRACKS

She'll cry them all into the ground
As though sowing a field with pain.

—Victoria Amelina,
(Ukrainian writer and poet, 1/1/86–7/1/2023)

. . . to listen and react to what is happening in the moment.

—Wayne Shorter

By chance collisions and faint accidents. . ..

—Wordworth, *Prelude*, I, 589

The universe is granular, not continuous. . .. You see a multitude
of tiny particles mingling in different ways.

—Carlo Rovelli, *Reality Is Not What It Seems*

FOOTPRINTS: EIGHT TRACKS

Don't lose your head over it, someone says, but I can't help
beginning to think of Gogol's character taking a whole story
to search for his nose,
                        so I realize that, while our small talk
passes through us unnoticed everyday like cosmic neutrinos,

it's the tragedy here that is in danger of getting lost: nameless
bodies still hidden among the sounds and rubble in Kranastok.

I am writing this while sitting along the river listening to

Wayne Shorter's *Footprints* as he alternates between simple
and compound time, as if he were accounting for the waltz
flow of memory, and a future he somehow knew would be
tragic,
        the notes arriving like that river barge
on the Tennessee full of parts to fit some as-yet-unnamed
machine,
          just as these words are waiting for a poem,
                                                for the name,
Victoria Amelina, that docks here, whose words offer

their own *field of pain*,
                          each image scattering in all
directions like electrons pushed out from their nucleus,

an image hiding another image—of scattered body parts,

———————————

so instead I think of the way Wayne Shorter would
push away from the melody because you always have to
travel beyond what the sound says

                                      and towards
the hidden scenes he'd imagine for each phrase,
                                      or
the way this river does not know where it is going, hiding
whatever lives beneath its surface,
                         or the spaces between notes,

or how Leonardo's work in Florence was covered over by Vasari,
or memories hidden in mass graves like a hive of yellow jackets,

which brings us back to the word *head* which I began with, which is
related to *hive*, which is why we can talk about thoughts buzzing
in our heads
                 whose ideas are like construction sites where
the blueprints don't match,
                              for sometimes we fear what we know
drifts away like my earlier versions, in a current random enough to

bring puzzling evening reports that are more like the huge question mark
the Webb telescope has spied about 1,470 light-years away,

which is not so far away as we might think from Victoria Amelina,

as I try to let all these sounds and words play at once,
                                      ricocheting
like shrapnel as they revise entire scenes,
                              questioning my ability
to understand, to honestly empathize,
                              because otherwise, as one
survivor said, *it seems like breathing the air from a balloon*
left by a dead man,
                         which is why it is so difficult to speak and yet,
as Cicero said, *to keep silent is to give assent,*
                                      and so I try not to focus
on the shifting river currents, or the egret's graceful swoop,

yet hoping, like Stephen Hawking, to find a theory of everything,

but in the end it is like trying to follow that reddening sunset
hovering around a buoy,
                            an image which only reminds me
of Amelia's *RIA Pizza* burning in Kranastok
                                        where a spotter
directed the Iskander missile, though all he saw disappeared
before he heard it.

———————————

                    In this way, Time loses direction: the past
won't stay past, despite the labels where we mark a date that has
expired.
                And when I look to my compass, the headings make no sense.

Like a bird in an empty sky, Victoria wrote.
                                        We were trying,
Wayne said, *to make a music where you don't resolve something*,
so that each time he played *Footprints*, as if imagining tracks
frozen in mud from another age, he played it differently.

And how much of what Victoria could have written has gone
the way of dark matter?
                            Here, as evening slides slowly over
the water trying to breach the other bank, the moonlight dappling
the surface into unread messages, I am trying to trace my own
footprints,
            lit by a moon that has been shrinking in diameter
some 380-odd feet since its beginning, which means it is pulling
less on the fluids in our heads each day, and so also our moods

which, most of the time, are as out of control as this poem's
improvisations into whatever key is at hand, which is just
a way to avoid the pain of imagining unspeakable details.

There are colors you can't see connected to the ones you can,
Wayne once said, changing tempo and pitch, the way
the barge's sound echoes off each building in different
keys.
      It's like Brownian motion where all the particles
fly about randomly then seem to make a pattern to start anew.

———————————

But to get at the cause, at or own beginning, as Stephen Hawking
shows, is where time turns into space, linking this riverside scene
to piles of rubble,
              and then the story of Victoria, caught by the missile,
recorded perhaps from a drone hovering in these white spaces,

which leads me to the ones those kids fly across the river,
unaware of history, playing their innocent game of war.

So maybe it is space, not time, that sweeps me along with all
these intersecting details leading to, to what?
                      What does it mean
to write this single elegy among so many deaths?
                  Maybe it's
a question like asking what these early stars are looking for?

Do you think they want to reclaim the light they lost?
And how do we know if any truth wants to be found?

The waterfall doesn't want to be listened to.

The egrets don't
care if you hear them.
With nothing as guide, where
do these quanta-like thoughts, that roam across the river
with those egrets, come from?
Some black hole of langauge?

For instance, what prompted Victoria to write about Hanna and
the tank planted in her garden,
an image involving everyone
who has lost everything, and meaning how a poem has to
traverse beyond memory to find what it will become.

Gogol himself gave up his *Dead Souls* by ending mid-sentence.

Wayne would sometimes stop and listen to the others play
before deciding what direction the band would take.

———————

I was writing all this amidst the news of that missile strike
at the restaurant in Kranatosk, a torture room in Bakmut,
a slaughter in Sderot, missiles into Ashkelon and Gaza,

a bombing in, well,
you pick the place for, like Heisenberg,
we can't be sure of any place and time.
There is just the debris
that settles after the bomb.
I confess: I once began all this with
that buoy swaying like a head in the barge's wake,
until I saw

that shadow of a head peering from the fallen building, and
then the portrait of Amelia.
                              When we look at our shadow it is
the head that is always the furthest away from us.
                                                    It has no spot
for the heart, nor the voices we should be hearing from among
the few scattered memories sifting through smoldering ruins.

Every thought ends up buried among the other thoughts.

No wonder all I find is a pattern that is forever deserting me.

This evening all I see, when I look up, is a canvas spreading out
from billions of years ago, before I had a stake in any of this.

———————————

Maybe, after all, there is a link I don't understand between
there and here, Victoria and all of us, between this peaceful
setting and the far horrors we see that are so hard to face.
                                                          Yet
it's as if every sentence tries desperately to ignore the others.

And that missile strike—tomorrow the news will gather dust in
the corner with the other memories.
                            Quantum waves rippling
through the grass down the slope in front of me have been
arriving since the beginning,
                            yet Hawking says there is no
beginning and I feel as if I am lost in that part of those ancient
maps labeled *Unknown*.
                        Maybe all this means that the real
world is an example of something we can't see.

Wayne once said
sometimes the rabbit runs down the hole and sometimes
he falls into it.

We'll never see the far end of the universe.

Pascal
wrote that we live between infinitely small and infinitely
huge worlds we can never see.

See how easily one emotion
telescopes away from another.

Maybe all these jarring
tones and moods are all we have to remind us we are never
really where or when we are.

Tonight I wondered about
the moment Jesus thought he might escape.

It's a moment
we all know.

It is like hoping that missile might have landed
in an open field.

Here, I am still watching the buoy sway
like a monk at prayer.

Maybe, as Leibniz thought, we need
to find words to put a lighter mask upon the tragic just to
survive,

letting us say what we thought we couldn't say.

————————

So maybe it is no accident that I began with the reference
to Gogol who was born in the Ukrainian Cossack town of
Sorochyntsi, not far from the bombed restaurant in Kranastok.

Victoria spent her last days reporting the war crimes she fell
victim to.

Before long we may need metal detectors to find
our hearts.
It may be that each sentence is a battlefield
of impossible solutions.
And as I hope now for some symbol,
some sign like the Cosmic microwave background noise linking
us all to our beginnings, to that Kranastok restaurant,
to our own lost selves,
I remember Victoria's own words, still
playing in my head—*There were silences instead of much-needed
stories, where there's a lack of true stories, there's a lack of trust.*

And I remember how the physicist Max Planck figured
God is everywhere present, that *the holiness of the unintelligible
Godhead is conveyed by the holiness of symbols,*
though
mine often means the world we live in is so often just a vision
in some funhouse mirror,
or like Narcissus listening to
his own echo always out of reach,
or like the fact that,
as with Wayne, there are only so many words between me
and my death.

———————

Victoria's unwritten words remain invisible
here among the daytime stars, lost forever,
for as Wayne
wrote, *clouds float in the same path only once,*
but maybe, also,
like that starlight voyaging out from its far side towards worlds
we have yet to include,

approaching where we all began,

or this

river searching for its beginning in its end.

As *Footprints'* lyrics go:

we touch on the past now, to show us where to go,

maybe the next

poem, or a tentative prayer to whatever connects us, an impossible
theory of everything,

which is why I must end this elegy with a comma,

III

AGAINST OUR WINTERS

Under each station of the real,
another glimmers.

—Jane Hirshfield, "If the Truth Is a Lure. . ."

Lo sai la polvere non cade, ma si alza

—Antonella Anedda, "Povria" *Historiae*
(You know that dust does not fall, it rises)

We know he looks at us like all the stars. . .

—Delmore Schwartz, "Starlight Like Intuition. . ."

There Is in all visible things, an invisible fecundity,
a dimmed light, a meek namelessness, a hidden wholeness.

—Thomas Merton

ELEGY TRYING TO BE A PSALM

For Wilbur

Because it is not here it is eternal
   —W.S. Merwin

Crows imitating human voices, a Field Sparrow
imitating a cricket, Blue Jays imitating hawks
Catbird, Cattle Egret, Snail Kite, Herring Gull,

sometimes it seems everything is filled with
other spirits, as the Cherokee know.
                                          This evening,
it was not the hawk smudging past me, then
slicing into the trees,
                          but your soul reminding me
we are always moving elsewhere.
                                    *The dead
are invisible*, not absent, St Augustine wrote.

We know this the way we see sounds and hear
colors, the way we never see the plane whose
distant hum points us to its past,
                                 or the seed
ready to flower at our feet.
                          In this way
nothing is ever finished.
                          In Milano once, I wept
for Michelangelo's Pieta Rondanni, two figures
trying to escape the stone the master abandoned,
two souls he still inhabits
                          as a repeated dream
that seems, somehow, to still chip away at the air.

I think this hawk has waited on the porch post for
me to say or do something he already suspects.

I would like to tell you what has happened since
you left,

but it is enough now to speak to these
souls reminding us they are not simply what we see—

the speckled moth I just mistook for a butterfly,

the whole galaxy moving away but taking us
with it,
      the invisible day stars,
                    the mourning doves
taking over for the owls,
          and these words for you,

always waiting for what is always arriving.

JUBAL'S SONG

. . . he was the first of all who play
the harp and the flute.
           —Genesis, 4:21

I was born in an age of black stars, a cratered sky,
tracing the worn paths of meteors, listening to
the bones of lost planets,
                             yet even in that time,
after the garden wall had long crumbled, I could
see the wind singing through the trees, hear
the news each astonishing sunrise brings, feel
the undulating wave of swifts each evening.

I learned from bird song, from the rippling stream,
the thrum of insects, even the howl of wolves.

It was a music, no, a language there are no words for,
a poem of consolation, a world you must discover
the way you see again those dried riverbeds from the sky,
or the way the wind remembers everything it has touched.

Think of the way mushrooms live in the dead tree.

Think of the way these moths will die for the light.

I know, you think I am speaking a language of things
that no longer exist.
                    I have been to your world:
it is like the turtle that cannot right itself.
                                  So many
minds are just so much tangled underbrush.

Serpents posing as leaders, false prophets leading you
to messiahs of hate, mass graves filled with lost
dreams, a world that is the mutilated landscape
of your own souls.
                    How easy to simply turn as the hawk
turns, to see how everything is linked, how the redwood's

roots entangle with those of other trees for support,
the way some ants feed on, yet protect, the wattle bush,

even the way these words have come together on this page.

Anything is possible in this world where there are animals
with ears in their knees, noses on their limbs or eyes
on their genitals.
                    You only have to look.
                                        Nothing is foreign.

You have your own poets though few have listened.

Still, as long as there is language there is hope.

Each word whispers a way to cross its own horizon.

Each poem contains the echo of every sound that was,

consoles the way a standing pool consoles the rapids.

Just listen. Here is a new sound this evening.
                                        It is coming
from the forest, or perhaps it has come from you.

It has slipped between the two sides of the wind.

It is like the sound of one leaf kissing another as it falls.

AGAINST OUR WINTERS

The world was already here,
Serene in its otherness
      —Charles Simic, "Late Arrival"

You'd have noticed the turtle in my garden first.

When the dog noses around, it hides inside its own
dome of constellations.
                The *Flammarion*
Engraving shows a man crawling under
the edge of the sky's shell in an attempt
to reach eternity.
                  It was Aristotle who
claimed the dome of heavens above us was
a perfect geometric figure we couldn't breach.

It's an idea some say he borrowed from
Africa.
            One night you suggested Dexter's
"A Night in Tunisia" from *Our Man in Paris*,
when everything seemed to be falling apart.

The stars are aglow in its heavens,
you would have said of our turtle.

I think it must be a supreme astronomer.

Turtles have been around since the Miocene.

Since then the stars have shifted place—
out of those galactic orchards, as you
called them, that night on Hampton Beach,

the sea losing itself in the sky at the far horizon.

Still *the moon is the same moon above you*
is what you'd tell us now, maybe humming it
because all *words fail*, as the tune goes.

Too often, we too, are exiled from our own
words, trying to crawl out from under
our own lives.
                    As today, a day not knowing
it is dying, thinking to continue under its own
stars, the moon opening like a wound in the sky,
later to be swallowed by distant black holes,

though we know *the truth is dark under your
eyelids*, as you wrote, themselves a kind of
shell revealing eternity's quick and aimless glance,
where, nevertheless, *the stars are aglow in the heavens.*

SAVING THE LAST DANCE FROM LAMBERTVILLE

for we lived mostly in the understories. . .
—Gerald Stern

So what if those stars had long ago become
cinders,
        we still believe what we see, still read
our lives by them.
              So what if we say it really was
the crows that pulled this darkness over us,
                          or
that the mockingbird was singing only for us,

that the Leonids wrote a few quick lines to you across
the dark.
        Every metaphor is a truth just out of reach.

And so what if we say the sound painted the walls,
or your words touched us with their soft hands,

for we were stars ourselves, galaxies spinning,

dancing around the kitchen with you chanting
Mingus' *Eat That Chicken*,
                telling stories whose
truth never mattered, but flashed like meteors,
singing out of tune, half hoarse, half saxophone,

and, yes, those stories sliding from the shelves of
memory,
        and didn't we want to believe your opossum
really was Lazarus?
          And you?
             Tonight, I put on
Oh Yeah, listening to the whole band join in,
Eat that Chicken, Eat that Chicken Pie,
the whole cosmos was spinning around them

which brings me to that star, L 1527, being
born again in the Webb telescope's lens eons ago,
and now, but also far into its own future, a kind of

chant itself, a kind of prayer, that returns us to a time
we all lived, as you did, *partly underground,*

                                 as if practicing
to resurrect ourselves in dance, in chants, with memories
almost out of reach,
                   but for those few words we repeated
as if repeating the lives we wanted them to fill once again,

those loves you've never let turn to cinders or to darkness.

GHOST FORESTS

The Trees Will Die
   —Robert Pack

I dreamed we both moved through a windy mist,
lost on a Carolina salt marsh, guided by wisps
blinking ahead of us like fireflies.
                          Constellations
we couldn't recognize rose out over the closing
sea.
    Stripped trunks of tree, and stumps like blunt
thorns spotted the water, ghost forest they call it,
for woodlands the rising seas have claimed.

There's a carapace of lies to deny the ends of things.

Your dream was to merge your words with trees.

I think your tamarack knew how to begin again.

How can we know what a salt marsh means to say?

Here, it's the blur of notes from the marsh wren.

There, it's the whistle through the dying white pine,
their shadows' shadows disappearing with the seeds
the birds need.

           It's our own ends we see ghosted now,
as your own end ending until it ended, a kind of song
that only the trees, linked through their roots, must know.

What happens then depends on what we believe—
maybe in the tamarack, or in sudden wisps of light
we can't explain, *this world of worded things*
whose ghostly echoes both warn us and console.

Carolina, Montana

NOCTURNE

What but design of darkness to appall?
　　　—Robert Frost, "Design"

The Red Tail screams its accusations through the haze of
smog and drizzle above the power plant,
　　　　　　　　　　　　　　slides to an oak
branch where it opens its wings to dry and cleanse.

The memory of an extinct bird flutters in the underbrush.

I am listening to the tree frogs recite their endless lectures.

As the haze burns off the sun begins to set:
　　　　　　　　　　　　　　the more intense
the color, the more polluted the air.
　　　　　　　　　　　　We don't really have
a name for that more than its false beauty.
　　　　　　　　　　　　　On some walks
we see no tracks, hear no birds or insects.
　　　　　　　　　　　　　It's the darkness,
not a deer, that rises from the underbrush.
　　　　　　　　　　　　　It's bottles that
outnumber the fish in Chickamauga Creek.
　　　　　　　　　　　　　If only we could
cradle the earth in our arms.
　　　　　　　　　　　　I am watching the squirrels
drop chestnut pieces onto the drive so that the sparrows
will pick up the scraps,
　　　　　　　　　　　as later the racoon will clean up
whatever it can from our compost heap.
　　　　　　　　　　　　　　How naturally
one thing can speak to another.
　　　　　　　　　　　　We have so many words
for this, and so few that have taken root.
　　　　　　　　　　　　　　Yesterday
I watched a starling perched on the back of a deer,
picking parasites off its hide.

Today, someone burns
a rain forest, another spills something unpronounceable
into a creek.
What the Red-tail screamed, what
the tree frogs lectured, was that there is less and less
of their world that will, in the end, be there to forgive us.

ENCOUNTER

Hard to see with the cloud of gnats undulating
in waves before us,
                    the doe, too, nearly at arms'
length, too busy with the sweet grass between
the maples to notice,
                    the birdsong a faint prayer
inside the larger silence,
                    the night long done with
its secret business,
                    but us, unable to stir, stopped,
an open secret,
                    as the planet moved us for
whatever distance it spins in two minutes,
                    until
the doe stepped back a few yards, turning, questioning
something beyond her or our ability to say,
                    which
brings me to my own question: why remember this
now, why these words
                    except to relive the one
life within the two of us and beyond, a sacred
space, a kind of redemption, a sacrament of air.

Terri

KNOWABLE, UNKNOWABLE

I will hide my face from thee. . .
—Duet 32:20

The secret world under the turtle's shell.

                       The realm where
the whale dives unseen.

               No wonder our lost souls wander
around without us, clothed in rags.

                   Like children lifted up
to watch the parade just after the float passes.

                          To see
through not with the eyes, Blake once wrote.

                    Beyond whatever edge
of how we measure spacetime.

             What were You doing,

                    where,
before creation, St. Augustine asked.

              As if he could
eavesdrop on an answer.

             We are just the pause between
a pair of notes, Rilke wrote.

                Scarecrows pointing away
from ourselves.

          In truth, it's all a jukebox of desire.
As soon as you test one theory another arrives.

At this rate everything we began with will disappear.

We become like needles threading the last light,
our names woven in exile.

              Spinoza makes us
part of a huge watch.

            And now another theory
has comets bringing life to earth.

             Should I believe that?

The truth is, I don't know what to believe.

                                        Or I believe
every theory is finally an apology or a prayer,

and isn't every prayer a wish to be discovered or discover?

FORGET KEATS

What was the name of that bronze-headed god
in charge of the Temple of Distraction?
    —Tony Hoagland

No, not set in any country bower, and not listening
to some Nightingale tempt me with your immortality,

not even Lee Konitz and Warne Marsh playing
"Don't Squawk," with Marsh sauntering through
one long measure after another, as if they could
put off the end.
               No, this is *distractive poetics*,
moving from the highway sounds at the ridge
cut, to the neighbors' dog taunting the mailman,
to cicadas just starting to test their own songs
against some Blue Jay's refusal to return to its nest.

Don't squawk, don't complain, my father said
when my friend died, *just remember*, placing
another 78 on the turntable—
                   Benny Goodman's
Ballad in Blue, as I remember, as it lifted my father
away from his own brother's plunge in a B-17
into Belgium.
            Why do so many elegies mention music?
It gives soul to the universe, wings to the mind,
Plato wrote.
           The point is, so many things keep
dying, going silent, which means we all have to make
our nests amidst the thorns,
                  trying to find the right
notes for the butterfly inspecting our fingertips
or today's rain still dripping reluctantly
from the branch,
           so maybe it's time to refuse any poem
that begins with an allusive lament or regret.

So forget Keats, forget mourning—what does that
squawking jay have against me sitting here remembering you?

NOT FACING IT

Once you get close enough, you see what
one is stitching is a human heart.
I don't know what people mean by reality.
                    —Dean Young

The day's news arrives without invitation
                              but *Time's*
arrow has two points, you once quipped, the way
a tune walks around in your head until you don't
know where it begins or ends.
                         Or one chord
falls unexpectedly into another,
                         as Nels Cline's
guitar slides up and down the heart's strings
behind Ron Miles' trumpet,
                         and you have to
find a way to get back
                    with whatever image
comes jarringly to mind, like that crow who
just returned to the carcass after the car slid by.

That's why we ransack reality for alternative visions
the way groups of stars pretend to be constellations,

or the way that street preacher megaphones his revelations,
though no one's listening.
                    Riffing your poems, Ben Goldberg's
Reality seems to nose around in your words, his clarinet
slowly lifting up one reality after another,
                              then you respond
until you both eclipse, well, nothing at all.
                              I rewind emptiness,
you once wrote. *Reality is the persistent illusion* (Einstein).

It's all improvisation you'd have said, your own lines
riffing in whatever direction they want to, until you ask
How'd we get here?
                    I think you knew we are always mid-stream,
that there are too many lost, or crossed out, or un-played notes,
those *Phantom Pains* Goldberg blew his way through.

Imagination's music can take us anywhere, but for a price,
as when the heart so often betrays us.

MALCHUS' ACCOUNT: THE BETRAYAL

Matthew 26:51

The garden wavered in the torchlight, but not Him.

Why we brought weapons? Well, I never understood.

I feel I am walking over a bridge suspended between
then and now.
    What were we afraid of?
         Being a slave,
I overheard all their secrets and how they lied to us.

You that have ears, I heard Him say once, and now
I understand.
    The others argued over what to call
Him, but the stars don't care what name we give them,
and turn to more important business.
        See, now I am
sounding like Him and his little stories. I live in a story
that already seems to have its ending.
        Each word of His
brings its own world.
    When you lose your hearing,
even for a moment, it is not the pain, not the desire
for revenge—all you want to hear afterwards is the truth.

It has nothing to do with the glitter of gold or power.

It has to do, as I saw that night, with the way that
Turtle-Dove remained so still while the trees wavered.

THE WATCHMAN'S FEAR

I mean my words just so.
They're dark to those in the dark: not to those in the know.
  —Sophocles, the Watchman in *Agamemnon*

You too, must feel it, for it lands like a spear, the dreaded
light from the last signal fire.
                    It screams a silent scream,
the scream of falling stars, the stare of the buzzard.

We thought he'd perished with the rest, but now we both
fear and hope for what might happen next—if he brings
back the hate of the wolf, the lies of the goddess Apate,
the destructions of Perses.
                    Already these fears resemble
bees fluttering around the nest, desperate to hide.

Some ships have left the harbor.

                    The birds have already
fled, except perhaps the vultures
                    I want to remember
the streets that caried our futures, the vineyards that
once rejoiced.
            What he left, and may bring, is death
and betrayal, lives tunneled by hate.
                    Here I watch
horses grazing, pine trees weaving a canopy, but
beyond, a town turning on itself where so many
seem duped to believe that strife means strength.

Now I no longer know if I myself am watched.

You too must feel it.
            No age escapes it. None.

The stars have begun to shut their eyes, the clawed
feet of the wind have begun to work on me, there's
a full moon wiped clean by approaching clouds,
dolphins refusing to surface.
                    I know these signs.

I pray to the gods his ship will falter yet.

OUT OF THE DEPTHS

From the bottom of the lungs these words
whose meanings search for the unknown,

from ravines of doubt scooped out from
the Cumberlands,
                    from the chasms of fear pocking
the Dolomites,
                these clefts in courage, these
depths of despair,
                from under these fog-bound
Smokies hiding their own truths.
                          How often
we find ourselves in dead-end alleyways,

mistaking policy for belief,
                    caves for gates.
Or the way the sea searches for its end
in its beginning,
              or how mountains claw
their way towards the sky,
                  when the night
window gives us back only our selves with
a dark Rembrandt background
                    finding
only the empty space a ring surrounds,

for how often we walk along strange paths
trying to follow dissolving footprints,

how often faith appears and disappears
like fireflies,
              like dreams that drip with
the rain from the tips of leaves,

                              the cries
of humpback whales sounding down into,
and surfacing momentarily from the abyss.

From all these, a cry emerges, like a yell
from the bottom of an abandoned well,

like nestlings calling for their mother,

but then, every once in a while, the gust of
a memory we never had,
                              the path left
by dead glaciers,
                    the momentary world
lit beneath our closed eyelids,
                              a light
squeezing its way through a thicket of
branches,
          the sparrow's *seee-chip*
telling us to see beyond seeing,
                              and so
our words for all this, like snowflakes
touching the earth, dissolving their shape.

From all these, from the sinkhole of the heart's
failing words, a shriek, a cry, Lord,
this, a prayer made from the breath of sighs.

DREAM LIKE THE OWL

As it slips from a branch folding the darkness behind it,
threading its way between saplings,
                                        at this time when
your hours blur,
                        for there is no horizon it has not erased,
including yours,
                        weaving histories you will feel but
not know,
                like the racoon, chin scraping the earth,
looking up, curious, under unnamed constellations,

for there is no story your owl has not stitched to the alarm
of rabbit or wren,
                        gliding on this patchwork of moonlight,
silencing the nightjar,
                                as now it stops, scans the meadow
from a fence post,
                        listens as you do now, for the sounds
falling from nests,
                        stares with you through the tangled
blackberry screen,
                        through its own history back through
the Paleogene,
                        through the mottled fabric of your sleep,

over the deer-drop of some careless hunter, which

startles you now, as you turn, half awake, feeling
your wings pushing out from your shoulder blades.

MY FATHER'S IMAGES

Its yellow breast splotching the dusk like a headlight in fog,
that bird, the finch, refused to leave the windowsill.

I think it knew how his brain was limping to an early death.

This morning a grosbeak called out for hours for its dead mate,
the brittle clicks rising from its red breast echoing only
itself, as if it could no longer suppose that the present
was anything but one image of the past calling another.

All he had then was his past.
                                 These images would soon
flutter off the way his brother did in the B-17 over Belgium.

I remember another night we watched the dusk ripple
across six broken geese some boys had lined along the shore,
split down their sad sides like burst hoses of car radiators.

It was the senseless cruelty that made him shiver as if
he wanted to tell me again what his own war had cost.

In those days his dreams flickered on and off like fireflies.

Absence ate at the air like moths.
                                 What happens
to our words when we lose them?
                                 Faint shadows
begin to blister these walls.
                                 I remember how, beside
a tidal pool, he showed me a sea dandelion washed in,
cauliflower-like, that dissolved into rice and shapeless
petals as I lifted it to hold in my hands.
                                 He studied
his own fingers as if they could grasp the past.
                                              One
cloudy night he said the stars were buried.
                                       I didn't ask.

THE TIDES

There was a time when any symbol would do—the boat
barely visible on the horizon,
                              or the Pelicans slapping
the water together to corral the fish towards their fisher,

or the way it is said they pierce their breasts to feed blood
to their young,
                    or how they spread their wings like crosses.

You can find them sketched on catacomb walls.
                                                      Perfect
symbols for fishers of men.
                              Once I watched in horror
as a Pelican scooped up a dole of baby sea turtles
floundering in the surf.
                        Beyond, now, a lone buoy
leans in the tide's direction.
                              Darkness, too, rolls in.

Our truths like abandoned boats broken up on the rocks

and marked with graffiti someone spray painted
in the hope of making something of nothing.

At the turning of the tide,
                              an instant of infinitude.

What it brings is the vast darkness of the sea, an
emptiness whose meanings only we can fill.

HESED FOR TERRI

Though the mountains be shaken, and the hills be removed,
yet my unfailing love (hesed) for you will not be shaken.
      —Isaiah 54:10

Sometimes when we dust off our old feelings
to ask again the questions that brought us here
we find they are the same feelings,
                              the way
a river may change course but is the same river,

or clouds seem to change the sky that is still
the same sky,
            or the way a word like hesed
tells, cutting through time's fabric, how we
should live.
          One night I listened as, in sleep, you
spoke syllables that I wanted to learn as my own.

I read once how Donne etched his lover's name
on her mirror so she would be reminded how
he was always a part of her,
                        and how Keats
took his lover's letters to his grave.

No wonder our words sometimes fail to reach
each other
              only to find their passports
cancelled, their trains delayed, their planes diverted
to places like suspicion or doubt.
                              Waking
now, watching the redbirds line up on the branches
to wait their turn at the feeder,
                              I am learning
their language which has its own history,

which is the language of wings,
                        and love,
a remembrance, like us, over distances and time.

RECIPE

for Terri

I do the cutting while she does the planning and mixing.
We are thinking of Chicken Tetrazzini, though that could change
along with the position of the moonrise and the Geminids
marking the sky with their cross-outs against the bare branches
of the winter trees that reach like roots hoping to take hold
in what they must think is the rich black loam of night.

There's a north wind pointing the zebra grasses towards
the south, a kind of counterbalancing we could learn from.
In this way we can anticipate a future as we anticipate taste.

There is another world and it is in this one, wrote Paul Eluard.
Change is here but it's the stopping that worries us. Floating out
above us are worlds that have been turned to spheres of cinder,
black holes turning into white holes, radio signals from the big bang.

But right now we are thinking wine sauce, peas, garlic, chicken,
cheese, maybe carrot or zucchini, tasting as we go, thinking yes,
we should go on tasting forever, adding some salt or pepper here
and there because it is more important to taste the moment.

Kant linked our sense of taste to our ability to understand the world.
Spheres of cinder?—where did that come from but from the way
we had been describing what our own world is headed towards
under the threat of rockets and drones instead of apocalyptic
meteors.

      You could almost taste death one soldier said after entering
a savaged village.
        And so we go on, hungry, trying to add something
of beauty to the world, however spiced with the renewed knowledge
of the fragility of each moment, each life as it reaches beyond itself.

REPORT FROM MOUNT EREMOS

Matthew ch. 5-7

the crowd were amazed at his teaching,
for he was teaching them as one having authority...

So many of us then we seemed to carpet the slope.
We couldn't hear at that distance but we heard.
We couldn't see where He sat but somehow we could
see. The waters seemed to still themselves in awe.
Above us, the few clouds stopped moving or billowing,
the sun brought not heat but relief, the gulls circled,
silent, as if waiting for instructions. Even the lilies
bent to listen. We had come up the dusty road from
Tagbha, from Capernaum, from Syria. He looked
like any of us, and in a way he said He was. He wore
no outer tunic and the dust covered Him. He too
had come a long way but from where He seemed not
to have a name. His beard was scraggled. Where we
were going we did not yet understand. What was said
could bring down an empire. Maybe it has begun.
We were told to be lamps, to be the salt of the earth,
to see someone else in the mirror besides ourselves,
but many of us were puzzled, walking away, fearing
to be poor, meek or persecuted. I see it is the same way
with you. The gates in any age are small. The waters
across the sea looked ominous. We are supposed to
tell you everything He said, and yet how hard it is to
speak or hear words beyond words, for what He said
you understood through your heart. You've read how
trees communicate through mushrooms underground
as if they were all one, how distant particles become
entangled as one. It is the same way for us, is what
He said. I'm not saying you should learn from me,
a mere echo, garbled at times, careening through
your own world, for there are too many people
I have hurt, but also I know well that it is yourself
you hate when you demonize as your leaders command.
That's when you become just the dust beneath their feet.
I don't know how this Way came to be or even where
it will take me, except it is someplace beyond the need
for horizons, beyond that little hill, beyond these words.

TWO DOVES

It was passed from one bird to another
The whole gift of the day.
—Neruda, "Birds"

How hard it is to live in another's dream.
How easy it is to close its door with our own.

One night, hearing you cry out in dream,
I could only describe *the sorrow*
of the horizon, that the sky had lost its *grip*
on the clouds, and thought how easy it is
to find words to deflect what we feel.

.

Even Einstein, perplexed, could only
describe how distant particles impossibly
connect as *spooky action at a distance.*

It's true, we want to connect with all that is
not us.
              It was Aristophanes who proposed
that we need to collect our other half, separated
sometime before our birth.
                                     I read once
how some scientists describe love as
a "quantum relationship," destroying and
recreating itself, the way Stephen Hawking
described the evolution of the universe as
hesitating for a while, then continuing to evolve.

The other day, thinking of these past years,
we talked about how sorrow and joy are like
both the rays of light and the shadows they cast
through the trees.
                          It was then we heard what
one called the morning dove, the other the
mourning dove.
                        I believe it must be both—
each note holding the other in one dreamt song.

Tonight, as if pausing to remember something,
the moonlight stops tilling the earth, the wind
stops fingering the leaves, and these words, too,
hesitate, far from the love they mean to say.

For Terri

FINDING PARADISE IN RIVER PRETTY, MISSOURI

When Dante finally arrived there he had no words
for it.
            The frog giggers in the river must think
their spotlight is their way to revelation.
                                    The dam's
been broke for years, the mill's broken wheels turn back
to a time before time, if they turn at all.
                                    The evening sky
still leans down over the ridge line as if it wanted to be
water.
            The river rubs against the ledge rock.
                                    Here we are
far from beheadings and crucifixions in what was once
the land of paradise, a word that came from the Persian
meaning *an enclosed park*.
                        They must have had this place
in mind.
            One trout tries for but misses the Jesus bug
that skates away.
                        At night the bats will take what the fish
missed.
            Plato thought we are born with a memory of Paradise.

Imparadise'd in one another's arms is what Milton said.

I think that owl wants to be the moon.
                                    He knows
Paradise is the life you've hidden from yourself.

THE WHIPOORWILL'S SONG

Because you heard me does not mean you heard me.

I embrace change and tell you what your own soul tries to hide.

When you dream of me, listen carefully, watch the way
the branches point. I'll tell you where your path leads.

There is no path that does not split off to something new.

You have to embrace the night is what my song says,
embrace the shifting shadows, the creek's diversions,
the way the wind adjusts the shape of my tree.

I am the messenger whose message is like
the ticking of pine sap on dry leaves.

Too often you only hear what you want to hear.

Ever since Aristotle and Pliny I was thought
harmful to goats—*goat-sucker* the English called me.

The *lonesome whippoorwill* is what Hank Williams
called me. Dickinson was afraid of what I meant.

It's true, I can capture souls as they flee the body.

Because of that I am never alone, though it is true,
there are fewer of us now for all the forests shrinking,
your dogs and cats at our nests, your insecticides.

But that is history and no longer anyone's prophecy.

When I am still, be warned, as the Cherokee know.

When I sing it is an echo from the upper world.

It is the song of your own lost and searching soul.

TRICKSTER

The Coyote is often the trickster in
First People's stories.

It's getting late and there are too many signs to
to decipher—
              the coyote keeping pace off to the right,
dipping in and out of shadows like meaningless
syllables,
        the secret architecture of the pinecone
I have been examining,
                  the long scribble of geese
writing their indecipherable script far above us.

It was the coyote who brought fire to the Cherokee.

The smudge of tracks gives no hint of who walked
before me on this trail.
               Beside me, the faint path
the Creek used for war and commerce intersects
with a few remnants of civil war trenches,

and the news keeps breaking in on the cell,
another drone attack in the Ukraine, deadly
protests in Iran, more shootings,
                     like the sound
a rabbit makes in the claws of the hawk, no,

mosquitoes we hear but never see,
                     and now this
skull, cleaned by insects, but of what? —opossum,
squirrel?
        The color of the air starts to turn, the trees
forget what has passed through them.
                  It is here
that the poem breaks apart, trying to reconcile
these symbols as if from some faulty thesaurus,
one meaning folded into another,

                                        and ends by
saying that once again Coyote has misled us
to protect what is sacred and unreadable here,
the land of the Keetoowah, the land of the Creek,
meaning *people of a different*, now hidden, *speech*.

AN ENDING OF SORTS

Eternity is in love with the productions of time.
　　　　—Blake

When you face the sun as it begins to slide down
the other side of the ridge, all that fills the eye is
light,
　　　and when you turn away the dark spots are
like the day stars just starting to smudge the sky.

What we don't see is a whole forest of desires.

A patchwork of deer trails leading to, to where?

Beyond, cylinders of hay line the field.
　　　　　　　　　　　　　　I want to
believe there is no end to this trail.
　　　　　　　　　　　　　Here, surface
roots write indecipherable messages in Kanji.

Branches write and erase their own shadows
with the wind.
　　　　　　As a boy I'd run a path like this
that fell off sixty feet on either side.
　　　　　　　　　　　　I should
have died back then.
　　　　　　　　One of us did.
　　　　　　　　　　　The past,
like these words, rises up from the mind's tunnels
as unexpectedly as voles.
　　　　　　　　　There is always a hawk
or owl whose shadow rakes the ground for them.

Just here, the path is marked with the tracks
of so many animals, as if, unlike us, they had learned
to live together.
　　　　　　Everything that lives is holy,
Blake wrote.

This evening, Venus, just now,
rises over Jupiter and I would like to believe
it is a sign that means *love over power.*
The redbuds
have started to reveal their own secrets,
The ginkgo is
waiting for the right time.
This trail is never the same
trail.
Branch fall, shifting glacier age boulders,
the field mouse nervous across my path, the opossum,
fear-frozen.
Here, nothing is ever in the wrong place
even when it is in the wrong place.
I would like to
believe that the end would be always just the beginning.

Or I would like, in the end, to be these woods.

We all live in the borrowed light of the moon.

ANANIAS OF DAMASCUS' STORY

Acts 9: 10-19

To be sure, I was afraid. After all, he'd ordered
so many to be killed. I heard only a voice saying
go to a street named "Straight."

                           It was as if there was
no other sound, as if the birds had vanished like dew,
as if blinds had been drawn across the sky,

                                and so
I went like a hound scenting a path.

                           The house was
modest, bare walls, a worn carpet, a couple of benches,
a paltry bed.

               He was praying.

                         The river seemed
to murmur with him.

                      He couldn't see and then he could.
He hadn't believed and now he did.

                         I can't explain.
I thought of the gecko changing color.

                     All I did was
to place my hands on his shoulders.

                     Just then,
a flock of swallows lifted as if by one hand then
flew in all directions.

                He said it was a sign.
Later, his preaching brought threats of his death,
and we lowered him in a basket one night through
a break in the city walls that wasn't there before.

I can't explain.

              Someone said it was like sending
the infant Moses off in his basket.

                     I don't know.
He certainly delivered us.

               After that, the hills seemed
to embrace the town, the sky a protective shield.

I tell you this because of what you have made of us,
of this place, this heap of rubble and embers.

The words to describe that only evaporate quickly.

Later, his own words fell like Spring rain.

The desert bloomed. There was a light more than a light.

I pray that you too may know the voice, for it speaks
to the soul as the rippling circles of fish in the river, or
the way the river itself brims over, the way the sky
seems to grow with every morning's sunrise.

It is the voice of an ember that only needs your breath.

BARTIMAUES' VISION

Mark 10:46-52

To be invisible. To be the pebble in your sandal.
To breathe the dust of those passing by, to breathe
their words. Always on the outskirts. To sit. To wait.
For the gate to open or close. The crowds passing
to or from the synagogue, the merchants mumbling.
And then that day in this city known for its sound
of horns and the shouts of armies. Sometimes it felt
as if I could still smell the embers and rubble.
I knew what they did not, that there is a world beyond
what they see. Not a world really, a presence,
the way I could hear the sparrow flip its tail,
the quail rising in waves that rippled across my skin,
the eagle's waves breaking the air above me.
What the crowd said hurt them more than me.
Their words hung like rags. I knew each group
by its scent, incense sometimes, or something
that must have come from spices far away.
It made a kind of broth in the end, a single taste.
Everyone is entangled as your own science says.
Which is why I think He knew I was there all along,
but you have to ask, to call out as the psalmist says.
Just listen to the way one raven answers another,
the way the night sounds create their own world.
There is darkness and there is darkness, but for me
all is light. In the end, it was not just about seeing,
but about being seen. And so I followed a way
that still opens before me. It's true, I still keep
to the perimeter. It's enough simply to know.
Since then I've learned that we are all living at the edge,
that we must answer those voices that have no words.
Since then I have learned the language of doves.

CONVERSATION WITH MYSELF DURING AN EVENING WALK ABOUT A TRUTH BEYOND WORDS

For it is not knowing much, but realizing
and relishing things interiorly, that contents
and satisfies the soul.
　　—Ignatius of Loyola, *The Spiritual Exercises*

You might approach the Jerusalem of the heart.
　　—Scott Cairns, "Hidden City"

This is my Church
　　—John Anderson, Mohawk, overlooking Sequatchie Valley

Moonrise, everything seems to bloom on borrowed time.

Still, the opossum climbs the gnarled tree at my approach.

The racoon follows its worn slender path through the weeds.

Under the footbridge the insects walk on the water as if
they wanted entrance.
　　　　　　　　Jesus Bugs we called them as boys.
Spirits, John would say.
　　　　　　　　Once in a while a trout rejects them.

It is easy to make up parables about this rather than letting it
settle on you like the spreading ground fog.
　　　　　　　　　　The early crickets'
hymn grows silent at my approach, but others far afield fill the air
with *responsives*.
　　　　　　　　Actually, there's more space between molecules
of air than what its atoms take up,
　　　　　　　　　　the home of the spirit.

It was Aristotle who wrote: *Nature abhors a vacuum.*

Black Holes emit as much energy as they destroy.

They waver like Psalms between retribution and love.

Deep inside the tree, black ants are burrowing a vertical shaft.
that will fell it.
                        For years, the miners only warning was
a canary they kept caged.
                              In the distance, dry lightning
signals nothing at all.
                         Ignatius hoped his method would
lead to truth.
                  For Huxley everything was true and false.

Why does your generation require signs, Jesus asked.

Blake thought his scattered aphorisms would show that
everything possible was an image of truth.
                                The spirit dwells
in you wrote Paul.
                    A child asked if the soul lives in any
special organ.
                  Someone claimed it occupies a certain number
of grams.
               Why is there something rather than nothing? ask the
Philosophers
               Is Dark Matter there to explain what we fear is
our own emptiness?
                    Writing was, in its origin, the voice of an absent
person, wrote Freud.
                     Helium 3 leaking from deep inside the
core shows earth formed inside a solar nebula from the Big Bang.

Eternity is in love with the productions of time, wrote Blake.

It took nearly half a century to find the *god particle*.

We think to tame Time by caging it in zones.

                                            Its frantic eyes
pace back and forth.
                        The melting glaciers reveal a history
we denied for so long.
                        The *wind* brings its history with it,
maybe prophecy.
                    It is *throat* literally, but *breath*, and so *soul*
in translation.
                    The Japanese maple has suddenly revealed
its leaves.
            It has started to color the air red around it.

This must be the way the soul awakens after its sleep.

In a few months it will sit like a star, a red giant.

What are those dogwood blooms waiting for?

The mockingbird that flew against the window chased
its own image into the dogwood's reflection.
                                        Aren't we all
seeking a true image of ourselves?
                                In Your image
the text says, as our own souls begin to bud like
the supernova galaxy, G299 flowering light years ago.

Every star has its own sound.
                        These wind chimes add
their own sacred passages.
                            Everything we say
needs some further explanation.
                                Like what it takes
to turn a rock into a pool of water,
                                    the sparks from flint
into a waterfall.

Here it is all rosebay, Catawba Rhododendron
and Mountain Laurel.
Mt Pisgah looms at the end of the trail.

It means a mystery you can't attain.
Now, a far campfire light
from a place we've never been,
like the light that escapes
from a black hole.
Maybe a searcher's flashlight,
or the distant
headlights on a country road.
The light from invisible stars
that are yet to reach us.
Or this will-o'-the-wisp hovering over
the glade, as if signaling the way to some other world.

How can I not kneel down at this altar of creation in prayer?

Richard Jackson is the author of sixteen books of poetry including *The Heart as Framed: New & Select Poems* (Press 53, 2022), *Where the Wind Comes From* (Kelsay Books, 2021), *Broken Horizons* (Press 53, 2018) and *Dispatches: Prose Poems* (Wet Cement Press, 2022), and twelve books of essays, interviews, translations and anthologies. Other books include: *Take Five* (Finishing Line, with four other poets, 2019), *Traversings* (Anchor and Plume, 2016) *Retrievals* (C&R Press, 2014), *Out of Place* (Ashland, 2014), *Resonancia* (Barcelona, 2014, a translation of *Resonance* from Ashland, 2010), *Half Lives: Petrarchan Poems* (Autumn House, 2004), *Unauthorized Autobiography: New and Selected Poems* (Ashland, 2003), and *Heartwall* (UMass, Juniper Prize 2000), as well as four chapbook adaptations from Pavese and other Italian poets, and a chapbook of prose poems, *Fifties*. *The Heart's Many* Doors is an anthology of poems by American poets on the artists Metka Krašovec *(Wings Press, 2017)*. He has translated a book of poems by Alexsander Persolja (*Potvanje Sonca / Journey of the Sun*) (Kulturno Drustvo Vilenica: Slovenia, 2007) as well as *Last Voyage*, a book of translations of the early-twentieth-century Italian poet, Giovanni Pascoli, (Red Hen, 2010). In addition, he has edited the selected poems of Slovene poet, Iztok Osijnik.

He was awarded the Order of Freedom Medal for literary and humanitarian work during the Balkan wars by the President of Slovenia during his work with the Slovene-based Peace and Sarajevo Committees of PEN International. He has received Guggenheim, Fulbright, NEA, NEH, and two Witter-Bynner fellowships, a *Prairie Schooner* Reader's Choice Award, the *Crazyhorse* Prize in Poetry; he is the winner of five Pushcart Prizes and has appeared in *Best American Poems* as well as many other anthologies.

His poems have been translated into eighteen languages including books in Slovenia and Barcelona. His books and chapbooks have won numerous awards including the Juniper Prize, Maxine Kumin Award, Cleveland State Poetry Prize, Choice Award, Agee Award and others. He has given hundreds of readings and lectures in the United States and abroad, from Hong Kong to India to Israel and eastern Europe. He has taught at the Iowa Summer Festival, The Prague Summer Workshops, and regularly at UT-Chattanooga (since 1976), where he directs the Meacham Writers' Conference. He has taught at Vermont College of Fine Arts since 1987, winning teaching awards at both schools. In 2009 he won the AWP George Garret Award for teaching and writing.

He has edited three anthologies of Slovene poetry and *Poetry Miscellany*, a journal. He is the author of *Dismantling Time in Contemporary American Poetry* (Agee Prize), and *Acts of Mind: Interviews with Contemporary American Poets* (Choice Award). Originator of Vermont College of Fine Arts's Slovenia Program, he was a Fulbright Exchange poet to former Yugoslavia and returns to Europe each year with groups of students.

A Personal Note from the Author

Thanks to my wife Terri, who is also my best friend and reader, and for Ata Moharerri and Brabara Carlson for looking at earlier versions. Thanks also to the River Pretty Writers' Conference for comradeship and support, to Vermont College of Fine Arts, its faculty and its incredible students who continue to teach me as much as I hope they learn, and to my former students at UT Chattanooga who continue to inspire. Thanks, finally, to Pia, my secret editor.

.